STATES

UTAH

A MyReportLinks.com Book

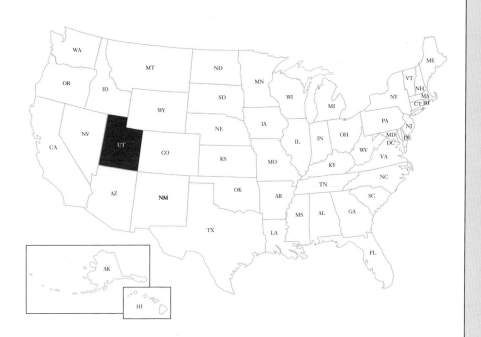

Stephen Feinstein

MyReportLinks.com Books

an imprint of

 Enslow Publishers, Inc. E

Box 398, 40 Industrial Road
Berkeley Heights, NJ 07922
USA

MyReportLinks.com Books, an imprint of Enslow Publishers, Inc. MyReportLinks is a trademark of Enslow Publishers, Inc.

Library of Congress Cataloging-in-Publication Data

Feinstein, Stephen.
  Utah / Stephen Feinstein.
    p. cm. — (States)
Summary: Discusses the land and climate, economy, government, and history of the Beehive State. Includes Internet links to Web sites related to Utah.
Includes bibliographical references and index.
  ISBN 0-7660-5097-1
  1. Utah—Juvenile literature. [1. Utah.] I. Title. II. Series. States
(Series : Berkeley Heights, N.J.)
F826.3.F45 2003
979.2—dc21
                            2002014853

Printed in the United States of America

10 9 8 7 6 5 4 3 2 1

To Our Readers:
Through the purchase of this book, you and your library gain access to the Report Links that specifically back up this book.
The Publisher will provide access to the Report Links that back up this book and will keep these Report Links up to date on **www.myreportlinks.com** for three years from the book's first publication date.
We have done our best to make sure all Internet addresses in this book were active and appropriate when we went to press. However, the author and the Publisher have no control over, and assume no liability for, the material available on those Internet sites or on other Web sites they may link to.
The usage of the MyReportLinks.com Books Web site is subject to the terms and conditions stated on the Usage Policy Statement on **www.myreportlinks.com**.
In the future, a password may be required to access the Report Links that back up this book. The password is found on the bottom of page 4 of this book.
Any comments or suggestions can be sent by e-mail to comments@myreportlinks.com or to the address on the back cover.

Photo Credits: Amethyst Galleries, Inc., p. 28; © Corel Corporation, p. 3; © 1995 PhotoDisc, pp. 11, 16; ©1999 PhotoDisc, pp. 18, 19, 21, 42; © 1999 Corbis Corp., pp. 26, 40; © 2001 Robesus, Inc., p. 10; Courtroom Television Network LLC, p. 15; Enslow Publishers, Inc., pp. 1, 25; Getty Images, pp. 30, 32; Hugh Hogle/Rocky Mountain Elk Foundation, p. 23; John Crossley, pp. 36, 44; Library of Congress, p. 3 (Constitution); MyReportLinks.com Books, p. 4; PBS, p. 38; The Utah Museum of Natural History, p. 12; University of Utah Press, p. 31; Utah County Birds, p. 34.

Cover Photo: © 1995 Photodisc

Cover Description: Arches National Park

Tools

Search

Notes
Discuss

MyReportLinks.com Books

Go!

Contents

MyReportLinks.com Books
Great Books, Great Links, Great for Research!

MyReportLinks.com Books present the information you need to learn about your report subject. In addition, they show you where to go on the Internet for more information. The pre-evaluated Report Links that back up this book are kept up to date on **www.myreportlinks.com**. With the purchase of a MyReportLinks.com Books title, you and your library gain access to the Report Links that specifically back up that book. The Report Links save hours of research time and link to dozens—even hundreds—of Web sites, source documents, and photos related to your report topic.

Please see "To Our Readers" on the Copyright page for important information about this book, the MyReportLinks.com Books Web site, and the Report Links that back up this book.

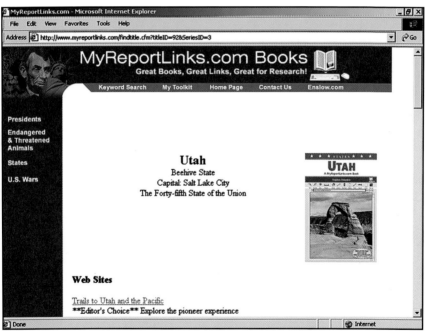

Access:

The Publisher will provide access to the Report Links that back up this book and will try to keep these Report Links up to date on our Web site for three years from the book's first publication date. Please enter **SUT5371** if asked for a password.

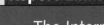

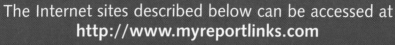

The Internet sites described below can be accessed at
http://www.myreportlinks.com

▶ **Trails to Utah and the Pacific**   *EDITOR'S CHOICE

This Library of Congress Web site tells the story of the pioneer
experience through diaries, photographs, and an interactive map.

Link to this Internet site from http://www.myreportlinks.com

▶ **Utah History To Go**   *EDITOR'S CHOICE

The Utah State Historical Society provides hundreds of articles related
to Utah's history. Learn about American Indians, pioneers, cowboys,
trappers, traders, and explorers.

Link to this Internet site from http://www.myreportlinks.com

▶ **Explore the States: Utah**   *EDITOR'S CHOICE

America's Story from America's Library, a Library of Congress Web site,
tells the story of Utah. Here you will learn how Brigham Young and
others went to Utah in search of religious freedom. You will also find
other stories related to local legacies in Utah.

Link to this Internet site from http://www.myreportlinks.com

▶ *World Almanac for Kids Online:* **Utah**   *EDITOR'S CHOICE

The *World Almanac for Kids Online* provides essential information
about Utah. Here you will learn about land and resources, government,
population statistics, the economy, and history.

Link to this Internet site from http://www.myreportlinks.com

▶ **U.S. Census Bureau: Utah**   *EDITOR'S CHOICE

The U.S. Census Bureau Web site features the official census statistics
on the state of Utah. Here you will find statistics on Utah's population,
economy, geography, and more.

Link to this Internet site from http://www.myreportlinks.com

▶ **Utah History Encyclopedia**   *EDITOR'S CHOICE

You can read hundreds of articles about Utah at this Web site,
including articles about people, places, and historic events.

Link to this Internet site from http://www.myreportlinks.com

 The Internet sites described below can be accessed at
http://www.myreportlinks.com

▶ **"Always Lend a Helping Hand," Sevier County Remembers the Great Depression**
Experience the Depression in Sevier County, Utah, through a collection of essays, photographs, and interviews compiled by high school students.

Link to this Internet site from http://www.myreportlinks.com

▶ **The American Southwest: Utah Guide**
The American Southwest guide to Utah provides pictures and descriptions of many national parks, including Bryce Canyon and Dinosaur National Monument.

Link to this Internet site from http://www.myreportlinks.com

▶ **A brief history of Sundance**
CNN provides a brief history of the well-known Sundance Film Festival, which takes place in Park City, Utah.

Link to this Internet site from http://www.myreportlinks.com

▶ **Crime Library: Butch Cassidy and the Sundance Kid**
Read a detailed biography about Utahn George LeRoy Parker, also known as Butch Cassidy, and Harry Longbaugh, the Sundance Kid. Photos of both are presented along with a detailed history of their lives.

Link to this Internet site from http://www.myreportlinks.com

▶ **J. Willard Marriot Library: Great Salt Lake Collection**
This photograph archive contains representative pieces from the Great Salt Lake Collection. Other categories listed include aerial photos, ethnic collections, Mormon history, outlaws, pioneers, and rivers and lakes.

Link to this Internet site from http://www.myreportlinks.com

▶ **Joe Hill: The Man Behind the Martyr**
This PBS documentary about Joe Hill tells the story of the Swedish immigrant who became involved with the International Workers of the World labor movement. While living in Utah, he was convicted of murder and put to death. This Web site documents his interesting story.

Link to this Internet site from http://www.myreportlinks.com

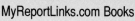
Report Links

 The Internet sites described below can be accessed at
http://www.myreportlinks.com

▶ The Mineral Gallery: Topaz

Learn about Utah's state gemstone, the topaz. View a photo of this
gemstone, and read about its chemistry, class, subclass, and uses.
A listing of physical characteristics is also included.

Link to this Internet site from http://www.myreportlinks.com

▶ National Park Service: Canyonlands National Park

Learn about Canyonlands National Park located near Moab, Utah.
This park preserves one of the last relatively-undisturbed areas of
the Colorado Plateau. View photos of this park, and read about its
cultural history.

Link to this Internet site from http://www.myreportlinks.com

▶ Native and Adapted Plants for Utah Landscapes

Learn about native and adapted plants in Utah. Included is
information about grasses, perennials, shrubs, and trees. Photographs
of the various plants are included.

Link to this Internet site from http://www.myreportlinks.com

▶ NBA: Utah Jazz Official Site

Read about the history of Utah's professional basketball team, the Utah
Jazz. Get stats and records of your favorite players, and read current
news about the team.

Link to this Internet site from http://www.myreportlinks.com

▶ Netstate: Utah

Brigham Young led the Mormons into what is now known as the
Beehive State. At this Web site you will learn interesting facts about
Utah and its people. You will also learn about Utah's geography.

Link to this Internet site from http://www.myreportlinks.com

▶ PBS: American Prophet Biography

About one sixth of the world's membership to the Church of Jesus
Christ of Latter-day Saints lives in Utah. Read about Joseph Smith,
the man who is credited for translating the Book of Mormon, and
the Church's history.

Link to this Internet site from http://www.myreportlinks.com

 The Internet sites described below can be accessed at
http://www.myreportlinks.com

▶**Rocky Mountain Elk Foundation**
The Rocky Mountain Elk Foundation works to ensure the future of elk and other wildlife, as well as their habitat. Learn all about the Utah state mammal. Sections include "All About Elk," "Hunting Heritage," and "Conservation Activities." You will also find elk photos.

Link to this Internet site from http://www.myreportlinks.com

▶**State of Utah Natural Resources Division of Wildlife**
Learn about the various species of wildlife in Utah. Choose from vertebrate and invertebrate animals, and plants. Included is information on Utah's state fish, the rainbow trout. You will also find photos.

Link to this Internet site from http://www.myreportlinks.com

▶**Stately Knowledge: Utah**
The Stately Knowledge Web site provides essential information about Utah, such as a list of state symbols.

Link to this Internet site from http://www.myreportlinks.com

▶**Still Pioneers: Utah in the 20th Century**
Read articles about twentieth-century pioneers such as Philo T. Farnsworth, the inventor of television.

Link to this Internet site from http://www.myreportlinks.com

▶**Today In History: Pioneering**
Today In History, from the Library of Congress, tells the story of Brigham Young traveling from Illinois to Utah with other members of the Church of Jesus Christ of Latter-day Saints, in search of religious freedom.

Link to this Internet site from http://www.myreportlinks.com

▶**Utah Birds**
Everything you need to know about Utah birds can be found here. Bird-watching places, rare bird-sighting reports, and a photo gallery of birds found in the state are presented.

Link to this Internet site from http://www.myreportlinks.com

Tools   Search   Notes   Discuss   Go!

Report Links

 The Internet sites described below can be accessed at
http://www.myreportlinks.com

▶**Utah Division of Wildlife Resources**
The Utah Division of Wildlife Web site provides information about
hunting, fishing, species, and habitat. Here you can learn about
conservation efforts and news related to Utah wildlife.

Link to this Internet site from http://www.myreportlinks.com

▶**"Utah Facts Book" 2001**
This is an online version of the printed 2001 *Utah Facts Book*. Here
you will find information on Utah's population, education, labor
market, transportation, government, real estate, public utilities, and
quality of life, as well as endnotes pertaining to the state of Utah.

Link to this Internet site from http://www.myreportlinks.com

▶**Utah.gov**
Utah.gov is the official Web site for Utah's government. Here you
will find links to living, learning, and doing business in Utah. You will
also find links to information about Utah's governor, Mike Leavitt.

Link to this Internet site from http://www.myreportlinks.com

▶**Utah Maps**
From the Perry-Castañeda Library you will find state, city, and
historical maps, as well as maps of Utah national and state parks,
monuments, and historic sites.

Link to this Internet site from http://www.myreportlinks.com

▶**Utah Museum of Natural History**
At the Utah Museum of Natural History you can explore the museum's
holdings and learn about current exhibits.

Link to this Internet site from http://www.myreportlinks.com

▶**Weekend Explorer**
PBS's Weekend Explorer takes a look at Kanab and Elk Meadows
in Utah. Here you will learn why these places have become
tourist attractions.

Link to this Internet site from http://www.myreportlinks.com

Utah Facts

Capital
Salt Lake City

Gained Statehood
January 4, 1896,
the forty-fifth state

Counties
29

Population
2,269,789*

Bird
California gull

Flower
Sego lily

Tree
Blue spruce

Fish
Bonneville cutthroat trout

Mammal
Rocky Mountain elk

Insect
Honeybee

Fossil
Allosaurus

Gemstone
Topaz

Mineral
Copper

Population reflects the 2000 census.

Song
"Utah, We Love Thee" (words
and music by Evan Stephens)

Motto
Industry

Nickname
Beehive State

Flag
Utah's state seal, enclosed by a
gold circle, appears in the middle of the flag against a blue
background. In the center of the
state seal is a shield. A bald eagle
is perched on top of the shield.
In the middle of the shield is
a beehive, the state symbol,
which represents industry, or
hard work. At the bottom of the
shield is the date 1847, the year
the first Mormons began set-
tling in Utah. At the bottom of
the state seal is the date 1896,
the year Utah became a state.

The Beehive State

Utah is located in the Rocky Mountain region of the western United States. It boasts some of the nation's most astonishing landscapes. Canyonlands National Park, in the Red Rock Country of southern Utah, is one popular choice for tourists. It is a spectacular region of canyons, cliffs, mesas, and plateaus. At nearby Arches National Park, visitors gaze in awe at gigantic natural stone arches. Bryce Canyon National Park features red sandstone spires,

▲ Called "Legend People" by the Paiute Indians, hoodoos are oddly-shaped rocks resembling goblins and other supernatural figures. These, as well as other rocks in Bryce Canyon National Park, have been formed as a result of erosion, mostly by water.

pinnacles, and strange rock formations known as hoodoos. At Zion National Park, the Virgin River has carved Zion Canyon with its 2,000-to-3,000-foot-high sheer rock walls. In addition to its many national parks and monuments, Utah has the Great Salt Lake, vast deserts, and impressive snow-capped mountains.

Utahns—Past and Present

For thousands of years, various groups of American Indians inhabited the area now known as Utah. The ruins of the Anasazi cliff-dwellers known as the "Ancient Ones,"

▲ In an attempt to preserve the cultural and scientific diversity of the state as well as celebrate its past, the Utah Museum of Natural History creates a detailed picture of Utah's colorful history with many collections and exhibits such as "Utah's First Nations."

are found throughout the southwest. In Utah, they are found in remote canyons in the southern part of the state. Another group, the Fremont, dug pit houses into the ground. According to photographer and author Chuck Place, "Fremont culture developed independently of the Anasazi, but the two interacted and their regions over-lapped."[1] Throughout the southwest, American Indian petroglyphs and pictographs decorate canyon walls. Petroglyphs are pictures carved into stone; pictographs are paintings on rocks. With both, the artists share something of their lives. It may be a hunt, a harvest, or a dance.

Utah has been home to the Ute, Paiute, and Shoshone tribes for hundreds of years. Indeed, Utah takes its name from the Ute. The origin of the word *Ute* is unknown. "It is believed it is an Apache word meaning 'one that is higher up' referring to the Ute Indians who lived higher in mountain country than the Navajo or Apache of the area."[2]

Only about 29,684 of Utah's approximately 2.2 mil-lion residents are American Indians. Many of them live on reservations occupying more than 2 million acres. Nearly 95 percent of Utahns have northern European roots. Their ancestors came mainly from Great Britain, Germany, or Scandinavia. There are small numbers of other ethnic groups as well. They include approximately 201,559 Hispanic Americans (mainly Mexican American), more than 17,657 African Americans, and about 52,253 Asians and/or Pacific Islanders.[3] The unique feature of Utah's population is that about 70 percent of the people are Mormons. They are members of the Church of Jesus Christ of Latter-day Saints. The Mormon Church influ-ences much of everyday life in Utah. It controls many of Utah's financial businesses, such as banks and real estate

firms. The Church is also involved in the state's politics and education.

The Honeybee

Utah is known as the Beehive State. When the Mormons settled in Utah, they called the territory Deseret. *Deseret*, a word in the Book of Mormon, means honeybee. The Mormons believe in working hard and making contributions for the good of their community, as bees do for their hive. In fact, Mormons regularly give one tenth of their annual income to the Church. This offering is known as a tithe. The church uses this money to help the poor, build chapels, and pay for the church's administrative expenses. Mormons also participate in unpaid community work projects. To Mormons, the hardworking honeybee represents their ideals.

This Is the Place

In the summer of 1847, Brigham Young (1801–77) and his Mormon followers arrived at the site of Salt Lake City. Believing his journey was over, he was reported to have said, "This is the place whereon we'll plant our feet and where the Lord's people will dwell."[4] In 1947, Brigham Young's grandson, the sculptor Mahonri Mackintosh Young (1877–1957), created Salt Lake City's "This Is the Place" monument.

Many people have felt that Utah "is the place." Author Zane Grey wrote *Robber's Roost* after spending time in the canyon country between Moab and Hanksville. The rocky canyons, known as Robber's Roost, provided hideouts for many outlaws, including Butch Cassidy (1886–1911?).

Utah writer Bernard Augustine de Voto (1897–1955) won the Pulitzer Prize for history in 1947. His award-winning

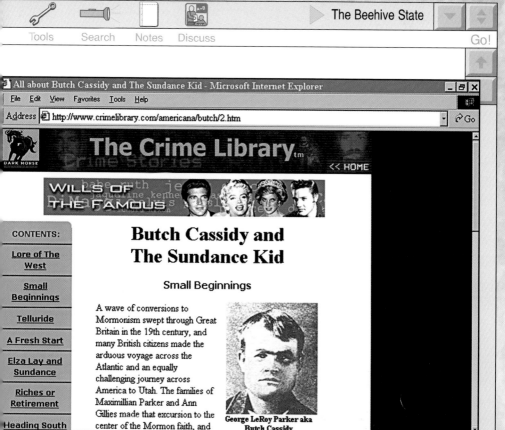

All about Butch Cassidy and The Sundance Kid - Microsoft Internet Explorer

File   Edit   View   Favorites   Tools   Help

Address http://www.crimelibrary.com/americana/butch/2.htm   Go

The Crime Library™

<< HOME

WILLS OF THE FAMOUS

CONTENTS:

Lore of The West

Small Beginnings

Telluride

A Fresh Start

Elza Lay and Sundance

Riches or Retirement

Heading South

Butch Cassidy and The Sundance Kid

Small Beginnings

A wave of conversions to Mormonism swept through Great Britain in the 19th century, and many British citizens made the arduous voyage across the Atlantic and an equally challenging journey across America to Utah. The families of Maximillian Parker and Ann Gillies made that excursion to the center of the Mormon faith, and

George LeRoy Parker aka Butch Cassidy

Internet

▲ Utah native George LeRoy Parker, also known as Butch Cassidy, was a notorious bank and train robber.

Across the Wide Missouri is about the Mormon pioneers. Pulitzer prize-winning author Wallace Stegner (1909–93) was born in Iowa and later moved to Utah.

A young Utah artist/poet named Everett Reuss (1914–34) fell under the spell of southern Utah's Red Rock Canyon country. In November 1934, Reuss, thirsting for adventure, set off by himself to explore a region known as the Grand Staircase. He never returned. Today, the legend of Everett Reuss continues to inspire Utah's young artists to finish what he had set out to do.

Land and Climate

The nation's eleventh-largest state, Utah covers an area of 84,905 square miles. Idaho and Wyoming form Utah's northern boundary, and Nevada borders Utah on the west. Wyoming and Colorado form Utah's eastern border. Utah is bounded by Arizona to the south. The southeast corner of Utah is known as the Four Corners. This is the only place in the United States where four states meet—Utah, Arizona, New Mexico, and Colorado.

▲ Canyonlands National Park is located in the Colorado Plateau region of Utah. The canyons and rock towers found here are characteristic of this region.

Utah's Three Land Regions

Utah has three main geographic regions: the Rocky Mountains, the Colorado Plateau, and the Basin and Range Region (also known as the Great Basin). Utah's Rocky Mountains are part of a long mountain range extending from northwestern Canada to Mexico. The Rockies in Utah consist of two ranges—the Uinta and the Wasatch. The Uinta Range runs east to west from Colorado almost to Salt Lake City. Other major ranges in the Rockies, including the Wasatch, run north to south. Kings Peak, located in the central part of the Uinta Range, rises to 13,528 feet. The Peak is the highest point in Utah. The Wasatch Range extends from Nephi northward into Idaho.

Utah's thickest forests are in the Uinta and Wasatch ranges. Just west of the Wasatch Range are Utah's largest cities, including Salt Lake City, Provo, and Ogden. Indeed, the Wasatch are so close they seem to be part of Salt Lake City's skyline. Nearby ski resorts, such as Alta, Brighten, Snowbird, Solitude, and Sundance, are popular with Utah's city dwellers.

The Colorado Plateau covers most of southern and eastern Utah. It extends across parts of Colorado, New Mexico, and Arizona. High plateaus reach elevations of more than 11,000 feet above sea level. The lowest elevation in Utah, 2,350 feet, occurs at Beaverdam Creek in the southwest corner of the state. Deep canyons riddle much of the Colorado Plateau. The canyons have been carved over millions of years by the region's rivers—mainly the Colorado and the Green. In addition to the canyons, there are gigantic, natural rock bridges and arches created by wind and water erosion.

In 1869, John Wesley Powell explored the canyons of the Colorado Plateau. The view at Grand View Point in present-day Canyonlands National Park amazed Powell. He wrote, "Wherever we look there is but a wilderness of rocks, deep gorges where the rivers [Colorado and Green] are lost below cliffs, and towers and pinnacles . . . beyond them mountains blending with the clouds."[1]

Utah's five national parks—Bryce Canyon, Zion, Canyonlands, Capitol Reef, and Arches—are located in the Colorado Plateau region, as is the Glen Canyon National Recreation Area. The region includes six national monuments—Natural Bridges, Rainbow Bridge, Timpanogos Cave, Cedar Breaks, Hovenweep, and Grand Staircase-Escalante. Rainbow Bridge is the largest natural stone bridge in the world. It is 290 feet high and 275 feet wide.

▲ The Mittens, located in Monument Valley Navajo Tribal Park, are composed of cedar mesa sandstone dating back to the Permian period, 270 million years ago.

▲ *Lake Powell was created when the Glen Canyon dam was built to hold back the Colorado River. This beautiful lake is a well-known tourist attraction as it offers sailing, water skiing, swimming, and other activities.*

Monument Valley lies within the Navajo reservation at Utah's southern border with Arizona. Its reddish rock formations rising up 1,000 feet high have been the setting of many Western films. Director John Ford's films *Stagecoach* (1939) and *The Searchers* (1957) featured Monument Valley. More recently, the valley has been high-lighted in many television commercials. Also along the Arizona border, but lying mostly within Utah, is Lake Powell. The huge lake was created by the building of Glen Canyon Dam on the Colorado River. Each year, visitors explore Lake Powell and its hundreds of hidden inlets.

The Basin and Range Region extends across the western part of Utah, most of Nevada, and into the eastern part of California. Much of the Basin and Range in Utah consists of extremely-dry desert. Level basin areas are separated by small mountain ranges. The most important features of Utah's Basin and Range Region are Great Salt Lake and the Great Salt Lake Desert.

Utah's Inland Sea

All that remains of ancient Lake Bonneville, a huge, 20,000-square-mile freshwater lake that covered much of Utah thousands of years ago, are Great Salt Lake and Utah Lake. Great Salt Lake is located in the northeastern part of Utah's Basin and Range Region. It is the largest natural lake west of the Mississippi River and the largest salt lake in North America. Its size varies between 1,000 and 2,000 square miles. The key factor is how much rain falls in a given year.

The water of Great Salt Lake is seven times saltier than seawater. The salt comes from the region's soil. Three rivers—the Bear, Jordan, and Weber—flow from the mountains into Great Salt Lake. However, there are no outflowing streams to drain the lake's waters. Each year some of Great Salt Lake's water evaporates, leaving salt deposits behind.

Great Salt Lake attracts huge numbers of birds. They feed on the lake's brine shrimp and the flies along the shore. About eighty thousand seagulls nest here. Also, millions of migrating birds spend time each year at the lake on their way north or south. Shore birds, waders, terns, waterfowl, Wilson's phalaropes, ducks, geese, and white pelicans are also seen at the lake—now a World Heritage bird sanctuary. Bald eagles are sometimes visitors as well.

▲ *After the Great Lakes, Great Salt Lake is the largest lake in the United States. It is the thirty-third largest lake in the world.*

Birds are not the only creatures drawn to Great Salt Lake. Many people come to the lake to swim or float. Even nonswimmers have no trouble floating in Great Salt Lake due to its high salt content.

▷ The Bonneville Salt Flats

Just southwest of Great Salt Lake is the vast Great Salt Lake Desert. In the middle of the Great Salt Lake Desert is a 70-square-mile area known as the Bonneville Salt Flats. The blinding, white land is so flat and empty that it is possible to see the curvature of the earth by looking at the distant horizon. The soil is so salty and so little rain falls each year that hardly any plants grow here. Still, the salt flats have value. Auto races take place at the Bonneville Salt Flats

International Speedway. Experimental cars are frequently brought there for testing. Rocket-powered cars have been driven there at speeds in excess of 600 miles per hour.

Jurassic Park

Dinosaur National Monument is located just east of Vernal, Utah. The monument, which straddles the Utah-Colorado border, is truly a "Jurassic Park." Dinosaur National Monument in the north and Cleveland-Lloyd Quarry in east-central Utah are two of the largest dinosaur graveyards in North America. Fossils from these two quarries are . . . being studied in museums and universities around the world.[2] About 145 million years ago, during the Jurassic Age, the area of present-day Dinosaur National Monument formed the eastern shoreline of a vast shallow sea. Land-dwelling dinosaurs waded and grazed in the swampy wetlands along the shore at the mouth of a river delta. Repeatedly, over millions of years, the river flooded. Thousands of dinosaurs would drown, and their carcasses became part of a sand bar at the river's mouth. The sandy muck eventually hardened into sandstone, preserving the dinosaur's bones as fossils.

More dinosaur fossils have been found in Dinosaur National Monument than anywhere else on earth. Earl Douglass, then-director for the Carnegie Museum in Pittsburgh, first came to the area in 1909. Since Douglass began digging, hundreds of tons of dinosaur fossils have been excavated. Scientists are still hard at work, uncovering dinosaur skeletons.

Wild Creatures, Large and Small

Dinosaurs, of course, no longer roam through Utah. However, many other wild creatures, both large and small,

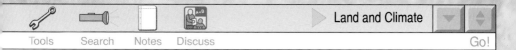

Tools   Search   Notes   Discuss   Go!

still make their homes in the state. The canyons, deserts, mountains and plateaus are home to antelope, bighorn sheep, coyotes, deer, desert tortoise, elk, kit foxes, moose, mountain lions, pronghorn, and ringtail cats. A herd of about four hundred bison lives in the Henry Mountains in the south-central part of the state. As many as three thousand wild mustangs gallop across the landscape in various parts of the Basin and Range Region. The horses are believed to have descended from stallions and mares that escaped from Utah ranches late in the 1800s.

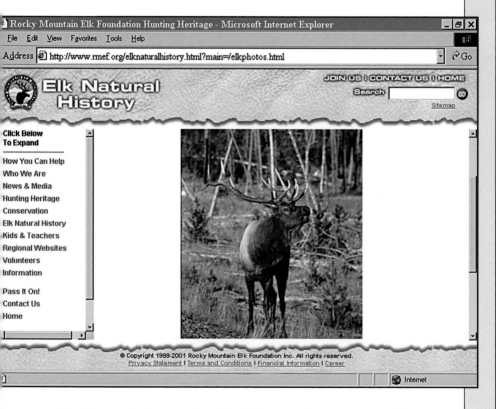

▲ In the early 1900s settlers killed off many elk, causing two of four subspecies to become extinct. The remaining elk are now increasing in number thanks to conservation efforts. Utah has the eighth-highest elk population in the nation and claims the Rocky Mountain elk as its state mammal.

The Greatest Snow on Earth

Ski-loving Utahns refer to the snow at their favorite ski resorts as "the greatest snow on earth." The dry, powdery snow is perfect for skiing. More importantly, there is plenty of it. Each year, more than four hundred inches of snow fall on the slopes near Salt Lake City. This is one reason that Salt Lake City was chosen as the site of the 2002 Winter Olympic Games.

In sharp contrast, desert areas located in the southwestern part of Utah receive hardly any snow. Annual precipitation in Utah ranges from less than five inches in the Great Salt Lake Desert to more than fifty inches in the Wasatch Range. In the summer, thunderstorms often occur during the afternoon in the mountains. In southern Utah, a sudden cloudburst can result in flash floods through the canyons. Writer Edward Abbey described what happened to him in Utah's canyon country on a summer afternoon:

"I have stood in the middle of a broad sandy wash with not a trickle of moisture to be seen anywhere, sunlight pouring down . . . the sky above perfectly clear, listening to a queer vibration . . . like a freight train coming down the grade, very fast—and looked up to see a wall of water tumble around a bend and surge toward me."[3]

Winters are cold in northern Utah but relatively mild in the south. Indeed, the southwestern corner of the state near St. George has been nicknamed "Utah's Dixie." Cotton is grown in the area. Average January temperatures range from 20°F in northern Utah to 39°F in the southwest. In general, winter weather is much colder in the mountains and on the high plateaus than in basins, valleys, and canyon bottoms.

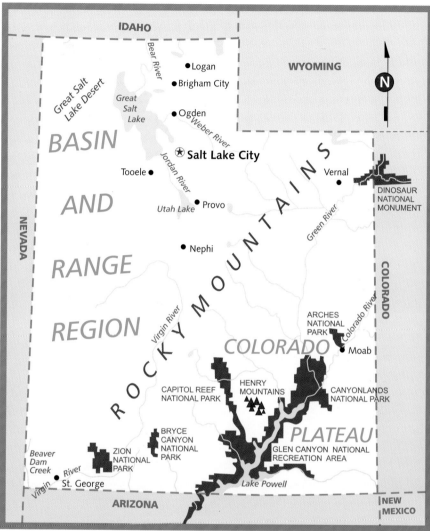

▲ *A map of Utah.*

Summer weather is usually pleasant in the north and in the mountains. However, the summer sun turns the southern canyonlands into a broiling oven. Temperatures often rise above 100°F. Average July temperatures range from 60°F in the northeast to 84°F in the southwest.

Chapter 3

Economy

In the early days of settlement, Utah's economy was based on the state's natural resources—what the land provided. The Mormon settlers' survival depended on how successful their crops were. They had to work very hard. As soon as they arrived in the Salt Lake Valley in 1847, they prepared the earth for planting. The soil was dry, so they dug irrigation ditches even before they built their homes. Before long, their efforts at farming the land proved successful. The Mormons built Salt Lake City, and then established farming communities in other parts of Utah.

▲ *Understandably, tourism is a major part of Utah's economy. In 2001, about one in every nine jobs in the state were either directly or indirectly related to the industry.*

The next phase of Utah's economic growth involved mining. This industry began in Utah in the 1860s when gold was discovered in Bingham Canyon. Mining became a vital part of Utah's economy. Copper, coal, and natural gas were plentiful. Railroads also played an important role in Utah's economy. They provided a way to transport Utah's products to market.

Utah's Diverse Economy

A varied mix of industries helps protect Utahns from a temporary downturn in any particular industry. Today, agriculture accounts for only 1 percent of Utah's economy and employs only 2 percent of all the state's workers. Mining now accounts for only 2 percent of the state's economy, and employs only 1 percent of Utah's workers. Manufacturing accounts for about 15 percent of the state's economy construction for 6 percent, and service industries roughly 75 percent.

Most of Utah's farmland—about fifteen thousand farms—consists of irrigated cropland. About 70 percent of Utah's farm income comes from livestock—beef cattle, sheep, hogs, chickens, and turkeys. Milk and eggs are important products. About 30 percent of Utah's farm income comes from hay, wheat, barley, corn, potatoes, and fruits such as apples, peaches, and pears.

Utah's most important mined product is petroleum— oil and natural gas. The state is the nation's second-largest producer of copper. The Kennecott Copper Company's Bingham Copper Mine, near Salt Lake City, is the world's largest open-pit copper mine. Utah's coal is especially valuable because of its low sulfur content.

Other products of Utah's mines include uranium, gold, silver, molybdenum, beryllium, and a solid form of asphalt

known as uintaite. The salty waters of Great Salt Lake are used to produce magnesium and natural salts.

Most manufacturing production is located in Salt Lake City, Ogden, and Brigham City. Leading products include aerospace equipment, state-of-the-art electronic products, communication equipment, medical technology, and scientific instruments. Provo is the state's computer center. Utah's factories also produce metals such as steel and aluminum, processed foods, and beverages.

Service industries are by far the largest part of Utah's economy. More than 1 million Utahns are employed in service industries. That is about 75 percent of the state's

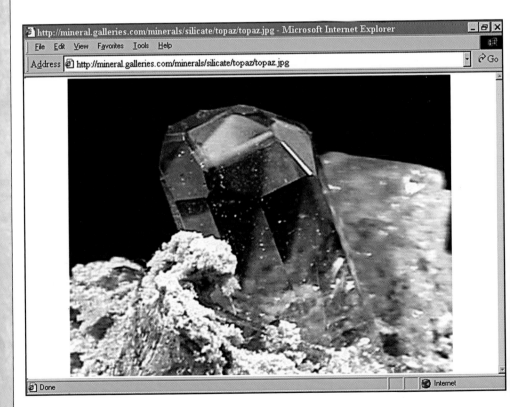

http://mineral.galleries.com/minerals/silicate/topaz/topaz.jpg - Microsoft Internet Explorer

File   Edit   View   Favorites   Tools   Help

Address   http://mineral.galleries.com/minerals/silicate/topaz/topaz.jpg   Go

Done   Internet

The topaz, typically brown to golden yellow in color, has been used in jewelry for centuries. This semiprecious stone is Utah's state gemstone.

workforce. Areas that service industries handle include tourist-related businesses, transportation, communication (telephone companies, newspapers, radio, TV), utilities (electric, gas, and water), and government (public schools, hospitals, parks).

▷ Tourists Flock to Utah

Utah first became a major destination for tourists in the 1920s. New highways made Utah's natural wonders accessible to anyone who owned an automobile. Tourists were soon flocking to some of the most spectacular sites in the Red Rock Canyon country of southern Utah. Since then, tourism has had its ups and downs. Yet, at the start of the twenty-first century, Utah was more popular than ever. Tourists spend more than $4 billion a year in the state. In addition to Utah's amazing natural wonders, many visitors are interested in the state's history. Salt Lake City, the state's center of culture and finance, is the most important historic site.

Each year, millions of tourists visit Salt Lake City's Temple Square—the heart of the Mormon religion. The area covers ten acres and is surrounded by a wall fifteen feet high. The various historic buildings include the Beehive House, Salt Lake Temple, and the Tabernacle. The Beehive House was the home and official residence of Brigham Young when he served as president of the Mormon Church and governor of the Utah Territory. The Salt Lake City Temple and the Tabernacle are the city's most important buildings. The temple is open only to church members in good standing. The other buildings in Temple Square are open to the public. The Mormon Church first used the Tabernacle in 1867. The Tabernacle is home to the famous 320-voice Mormon Tabernacle Choir. The choir

▲ *Set to the backdrop of the Wasatch Mountains, Salt Lake City was the location of the 2002 Winter Olympics.*

has given live radio broadcasts continuously since 1929. Today, the choir gives a live TV/radio broadcast every Sunday at 9:30 A.M. The broadcast is heard all over the world.

On the west side of Temple Square is the Family History Library, the largest facility of its kind in the world. It is free of charge and open to the public. People are welcome to visit the library to learn more about their ancestors. The library is run by the Genealogical Society of Utah, a division of the Mormon Church. The Mormons' interest in genealogy comes from their belief that the family unit, including ancestors, continues after death.

▶ Sports and Higher Education

Professional sports and higher education are also a large part of Utah's economy and tourism. The University of Utah, in Salt Lake City, and Utah State University, in

Logan, each have over twenty thousand students. Brigham Young University's enrollment tops thirty thousand. These institutions add greatly to the economy of those cities. In addition, people come from miles around to watch those schools' sports teams in action.

Utah is also home to a very successful professional basketball team, the Utah Jazz of the National Basketball Association (NBA). After drafting superstars Karl Malone and John Stockton in the 1980s, the Jazz became yearly playoff contenders, filling the seats of the Delta Center in Salt Lake City.

http://www.media.utah.edu/UHE/Pictures/p0000022.jpg - Microsoft Internet Explorer

File   Edit   View   Favorites   Tools   Help

Address   http://www.media.utah.edu/UHE/Pictures/p0000022.jpg   Go

Done   Internet

Brigham Young University was founded in Provo, Utah, in 1875 to give Mormon youth a religion-based education. Since that time, it has become the largest church-sponsored university in the country.

Chapter 4

Government

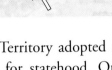

In 1895, the legislature of the Utah Territory adopted a constitution for Utah in preparation for statehood. On January 4, 1896, Utah became the forty-fifth state to enter the union.

▶ Utah's Constitution

Utah's constitution outlines the structure of the state government. It specifies the powers of the different branches of the government. It also describes the various powers of the state regarding such things as public health and welfare, public education, and natural resources. The constitution also prescribes Utah's electoral process. An amendment, or change, to the constitution proposed by

▲ Utah's capitol building (pictured here) is located in Salt Lake City. It is the state's second capitol building. The first, also located in Salt Lake City, was built in 1896 but was retired in 1915 when the current capitol was built.

the legislature must be approved by two thirds of the members of each house. The amendment must then be approved in a general election by a majority of the people voting on the issue. Amendments may also be proposed by a constitutional convention.

The Structure of Utah's Government

Utah's government is based on a separation of powers, similar to the federal government and the governments of many other states. The constitution divides state government into three branches—executive, legislative, and judicial. The executive branch carries out the laws; the legislative branch creates the laws; and the judicial branch interprets the laws.

The head of the executive branch is the governor, who is elected to a four-year term of office. The governor may serve any number of terms, but no more than three consecutive terms. The main task of the governor is to carry out the state laws. He or she must approve all laws that are passed by the legislature. If the governor vetoes a bill, the legislature may override the veto with a two-thirds vote in each house.

Other elected officials of the executive branch are the lieutenant governor, attorney general, state treasurer, and state auditor. The same term limits as the governor's apply to each of these officials. The executive branch also includes various state officials who are appointed by the governor. These include the executive directors of various state departments and members of state boards. The state senate must approve most of these appointments.

The legislative branch of Utah's government consists of a twenty-nine-member senate and a seventy-five-member house of representatives. The legislators' main job is to propose new laws. State senators are elected to four-year

terms. State representatives are elected to two-year terms. Senators and representatives may not serve for more than twelve consecutive years.

The judicial branch of Utah's government consists of the state supreme court, court of appeals, district courts, juvenile courts, and municipal courts. The state supreme court has five justices who are elected to ten-year terms. The judge who has served the longest acts as chief justice. The judges of Utah's seven district courts are elected to six-year terms. Local judges, known as justices of the peace, handle local cases involving minor disputes. In some communities, justices of the peace are elected. In other communities, they are appointed.

▲ *The California gull is Utah's state bird.*

History

Thousands of years ago, during the last Ice Age, thick sheets of ice covered much of North America. Sometime between 20,000 and 40,000 years ago, bands of nomadic hunters began migrating from Asia to North America. Following herds of animals, they wandered across a land bridge that then connected Siberia and Alaska. Sometime before 9000 B.C., the first hunters reached Utah.

▶ Utah's American Indians

The first people to inhabit what is now Utah are known as Paleo-Indians. The term *Paleo* refers to prehistoric times. The Paleo-Indians hunted big game such as woolly mammoths, bison, and saber-tooth tigers. After many centuries, most of the larger game became extinct. Descendants of the Paleo-Indians continued to hunt the bison and smaller game. About two thousand years ago, American Indians in Utah learned to grow corn. This led to a change in lifestyle. Hunters who had roamed the land now became village-dwelling farmers. Native peoples, such as the Fremont and early Anasazi, called Basketmakers, built adobe pit houses. The Basketmakers, who lived in southern Utah, became highly skilled in weaving baskets from plant fibers.

Later, about A.D. 900, the Anasazi began building cliff dwellings, resembling multistoried apartment buildings. These Anasazi were farmers who mainly grew corn, beans, and squash. They are known for their fine black-and-white pottery. In the mid-1300s, the Anasazi abandoned their cliff dwellings. Nobody knows where they went, or what

may have happened to them. Most likely, the dry climate in southern Utah became even drier, and the Anasazis' crops failed. Archeologists believe that the Pueblo Indians of New Mexico may be descendants of the Anasazi.

By the 1700s, three main groups of American Indians lived in Utah: the Ute, Paiute, and Shoshone. The Ute lived in the eastern part of Utah, the Paiute and Shoshone in the west. The Goshute people were related to the Shoshone. These natives lived in small groups. They hunted bison and other animals, and gathered fruits,

Utah Guide - Photographs of Zion National Park - Microsoft Internet Explorer

File   Edit   View   Favorites   Tools   Help

Address http://www.americansouthwest.net/utah/zion/zionnew2_1.html

▲ *Zion National Park covers about 150,000 acres. Many tourists stand in awe of the red and white sandstone cliffs that rise as high as 2,500 feet.*

berries, and roots. In time, all of these peoples faced a threat to their way of life—the arrival of the white man.

Explorers, Traders, and Mountain Men

The first Europeans to arrive in what is now Utah were Spaniards. Juan Maria de Rivera and his expedition are believed to have reached southeastern Utah in 1765. The Spaniards were not interested in making settlements in Utah. Instead, they wanted to trade with the American Indians. Spanish traders visited the Ute at Utah Lake. They gave the Ute blankets, kettles, guns, alcohol, and horses in exchange for furs. Possession of horses and guns brought changes to the Ute way of life. It made hunting easier and gave the tribe advantages over their enemies.

Early in the 1800s, American fur traders and trappers began exploring Utah. Many of them lived alone in the wilderness and learned the languages of their American Indian neighbors. These rugged individuals were known as mountain men. In 1824, mountain man Jim Bridger (1804–81) became the first-known white person to see Great Salt Lake.

In 1821, Mexico won its independence from Spain. Mexico then took control of Spain's former lands in North America. These vast lands were little traveled and hard to defend. By mid-1846, the United States and Mexico were at war over border disputes. In 1848, the Mexican-American war ended in Mexico's defeat. Mexico signed the Treaty of Guadalupe-Hidalgo, giving its vast northern territories to the United States. The states of Arizona, California, Colorado, Nevada, New Mexico, and Utah would come from these territories.

The Mormons

In 1830, Joseph Smith (1805–44) published the Book of Mormon. In it, Smith described a series of visions revealed to him by an angel named Moroni. According to Smith, the Book of Mormon was intended as a new book of the Bible. That same year, Smith established the Church of Jesus Christ of Latter-day Saints in Fayette, New York. Smith served as the first president of the Mormon Church.

Many people did not welcome the new religion. Smith and his followers moved from place to place during the next few years. In 1843, word got out that the Mormon Church allowed men to have more than one wife at

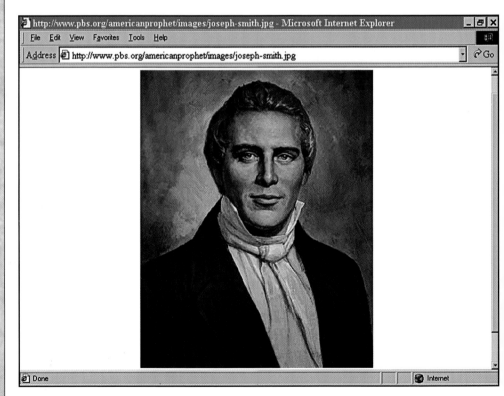

http://www.pbs.org/americanprophet/images/joseph-smith.jpg - Microsoft Internet Explorer

File Edit View Favorites Tools Help

Address http://www.pbs.org/americanprophet/images/joseph-smith.jpg Go

Done Internet

△ Joseph Smith, Jr., was the founding president of the Church of Latter-day Saints. He organized the Mormon religion in April 1830.

the same time. This practice is known as polygamy. Non-Mormons were outraged. In 1844, Joseph Smith and his brother, Hyrum, were arrested in Carthage, Illinois. Before they could stand trial, an angry mob broke into the jail and murdered the two men.

Brigham Young became the second president of the Mormon Church. By this time, about twenty thousand Mormons had settled in Nauvoo, Illinois. In 1846, Young led the Mormons to Nebraska, where they set up a temporary settlement. He then headed west with a small party to find a permanent home for the Mormons. The party included 143 men, 3 women, and 2 children. When Young arrived at the Salt Lake Valley in 1847, he knew he had found the place. Young hoped the Mormons would find here the religious tolerance and freedom they sought.

At first, the Mormons did find peace. They farmed the land, built homes, and began the construction of Salt Lake City. Many of the twenty thousand Mormons still living in Nebraska arrived in Salt Lake City during the next few years. In 1849, the Mormons in Utah provided food and lodging for thousands of miners and prospectors (called Forty-Niners). The miners and prospectors were traveling west to the California gold fields. That same year, the Mormons created a Perpetual Emigrating Fund. The fund provided money for Mormons emigrating to Utah. During the winter of 1849–50, Captain Howard Stansbury, an engineer exploring the Great Basin, stayed in Salt Lake City. He noted, "their [the Mormons'] dealings with the crowds of emigrants that passed through their city . . . were ever fair and upright." [1] He depicted their religious group as "a quiet, orderly, industrious, and well-organized society."[2]

As Mormon settlements spread to American Indian hunting grounds, some natives resented the newcomers.

In 1853, Chief Wakara (called Walker by the settlers) of the Ute attacked several Mormon settlements. Peace returned the following year, but it was short lived. War broke out again in 1865, when Chief Black Hawk led his Ute warriors against the Mormons. Other tribes joined in attacking the Mormon settlements. The Black Hawk War ended in 1867. The Ute lost most of their lands and were forced to live on a reservation in the Uintah Basin. Occasional attacks by American Indians against white settlers continued until 1872, when the Shoshone were driven onto a reservation in Idaho.

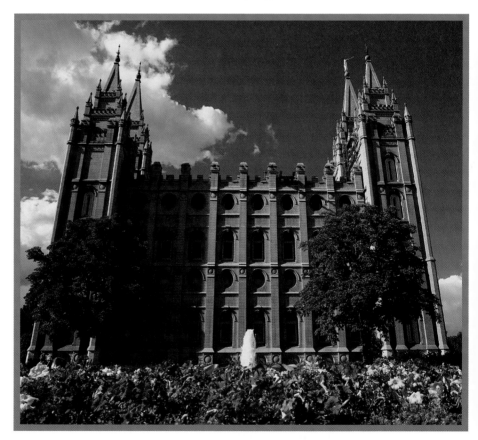

▲ Utah was first settled by the Mormons. Today, the Church of Jesus Christ of Latter-day Saints still influences the state's government and culture.

▶ The Quest for Statehood

In 1849, the Mormons established the State of Deseret. The same year, they sought to join the Union. Congress denied the request for statehood. It also rejected the name Deseret because of its religious link. Instead, in 1850, Congress created the Utah Territory, which included parts of present-day Wyoming, Colorado, and most of Nevada. Brigham Young became the first territorial governor.

During the next few years, the government in Washington grew increasingly unhappy with the state of affairs in Utah. In 1857, President James Buchanan ordered U.S. Army troops to Utah. The troops left Kansas for Utah in July. Their task was to put down a rumored rebellion and take control of the Utah territory. The Mormons, who viewed the advancing troops as an invasion force, made plans to defend themselves. In September 1857, a group of Mormons and Paiute Indians attacked a pioneer wagon train headed for California. It was rumored that the murderers of Joseph Smith were among the travelers. The Mormons killed most of the 137 members of the wagon train. This tragic episode is known as the Mountain Meadows Massacre. In the spring of 1858, the United States troops reached Utah. Shortly after, the Utah War ended.

During the second half of the nineteenth century, Utah's many petitions for statehood were unsuccessful. Polygamy was a major obstacle to acceptance. Meanwhile, Utah was becoming less and less isolated from the rest of America. On October 24, 1861, the nation's first transcontinental telegraph was completed. Telegraph lines from Washington, D.C., and from San Francisco, California, met at Salt Lake City. In 1869, the nation's first transcontinental railroad was completed at Promontory Point in Utah.

The railroad brought thousands of new settlers to Utah. For the first time, not all of the new arrivals were Mormon. By the late 1800s, only half of Salt Lake City's population was Mormon. In the 1880s, more than one thousand Mormon men were jailed for practicing polygamy. The federal government had outlawed the practice in 1862, but Mormons ignored the law. Finally, in 1890, Wilford Woodruff, then president of the Mormon Church, advised Mormons to give up polygamy. From 1890 to 1893, a Gentile (non-Mormon) government controlled Salt Lake City. It was time for Utah to apply for

△ Despite Utah's growing population and industrialization in the early 1900s, the state still managed to preserve its natural beauty. The Temple of the Sun, in Capitol Reef National Park, is one such treasure that has been protected by the federal government since 1937.

statehood once again. On January 4, 1896, Utah was welcomed into the Union as the forty-fifth state.

▶ A Century of Challenges

During the early 1900s, Utah experienced rapid growth and progress. The population grew, and the economy expanded. New railroads made it easier to ship products from Utah's mines and farms. A lack of water had always presented a major challenge to Utahns. Irrigation projects were needed to improve farm production. In 1913, the Strawberry River Irrigation Project was completed with financial help from the federal government. However, adequate water supplies continued to be a problem. Around mid-century, industry replaced agriculture as the leader of Utah's economy. Utahns understood that even more water would be required to meet the needs of a growing population. Early in the 1960s, several dams were built. Then, in 1967, construction began on the Central Utah Project to help bring water to dry areas. Work on the project continued into the twenty-first century.

There were other challenges as well. Although the 1900s would be a time of growth for the most part, there would be setbacks. American involvement in World War I (1917–18) brought prosperity to Utah's mining industry. The state's mines provided huge supplies of copper for the war effort. Nevertheless, Utah suffered along with most of the United States during the Great Depression of the 1930s. The state's mining and agriculture industries declined dramatically. Utah's unemployment rate was among the highest in the nation. World War II (1941–45) brought economic prosperity back to Utah. Once again, the products of Utah's mines and farmlands were in demand. Manufacturing also grew in importance.

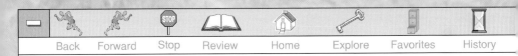

▷ Environmental Concerns

After World War II, the federal government established various military installations in Utah. During the Cold War, defense industries, such as missile production, flourished in the state. New problems and challenges arose in connection with certain defense-related activities. From 1951 to 1962, the United States military conducted above-ground tests of atomic bombs in the deserts of Nevada and southwestern Utah. Many years later, people who lived downwind from the sites of nuclear explosions developed cancer at an alarming rate. Residents of St. George and

△ The Green and Colorado rivers create three distinct sections in Canyonlands National Park—Island in the Sky, The Needles, and The Maze. This view is overlooking Island in the Sky.

other towns in southwestern Utah had been exposed to dangerous levels of radioactive fallout from the bomb blasts.

The military was responsible for other environmental problems in Utah as well. In 1972, the government admitted that the U.S. Army had been testing nerve gas at the Dugway Proving Ground in March 1968. A sudden wind had carried the gas in the wrong direction, killing 6,400 sheep grazing in fields in Tooele County. Utahns demanded an end to the testing and storing of chemical weapons. The safe disposal of toxic chemicals in Utah remains a challenge.

Most Utahns want to protect their beautiful state from the harmful effects of industrial pollution. The challenge will be to balance the need for industrial development with preserving the state's natural environment. In 1996, President Bill Clinton acted to protect 1.7 million acres of land in southern Utah from mining and other development. Clinton designated this area of unique rock formations as the Grand Staircase-Escalante National Monument. This and many of Utah's other spectacular scenic areas will remain unspoiled for the enjoyment of future generations of Utahns and visitors from elsewhere.

Chapter 1. The State of Utah

1. Chuck Place, *Ancient Walls: Indian Ruins of the Southwest* (Golden, Colo.: Fulcrum Publishing, 1992), p. 40.

2. Arlene Hirschfelder and Martha Kreipe de Montaño, *The Native American Almanac: A Portrait of Native America Today* (New York: Prentice Hall, 1993), p. 87.

3. Population figures are from the U.S. Census Bureau, Census 2000 Redistricting Data (P. L. 94-171) Summary File, Tabe PL 1.

4. Thomas Keneally, *The Place Where Souls Are Born* (New York: Simon & Schuster, 1992), p. 70.

Chapter 2. Land and Climate

1. John Wesley Powell, as reprinted by David Day, "Confluence Overlook," *Utah's Favorite Hiking Trails,* n.d., <http://www.utahtrails.com/Confluence.html> (January 6, 2003).

2. "Facts on Utah's History: Ancient History." *Utah.* n.d., http://www.utah.com/visitor/state_facts/history.htm (November 19, 2002).

3. Edward Abbey, *Desert Solitaire* (New York: McGraw-Hill, 1968), p. 120.

Chapter 5. History

1. Herman J. Viola, *Exploring the West* (Washington, D.C.: Smithsonian Books, 1987), p. 105.

2. Ibid.

Further Reading

Ayer, Eleanor H. *The Anasazi*. New York: Walker & Company, 1993.

Kent, Deborah. *Utah*. Danbury, Conn.: Children's Press, 2002.

Kummer, Patricia K. *Utah*. Minnetonka, Minn.: Capstone Press, Inc., 2003.

Marriott, Alice. *Indians of the Four Corners: The Anasazi and Their Pueblo Descendants*. Santa Fe, N. Mex.: Ancient City Press, 1996.

McCormick, John. *The Utah Adventure*. Layton, Utah: Smith, Gibbs Publisher, 1998.

Nash, Carole Rust. *The Mormon Trail and the Latter-day Saints in American History*. Springfield, N.J.: Enslow Publishers, Inc., 1999.

Neri, P. J. *Utah*. Danbury, Conn.: Children's Press, Inc., 2002.

Repanshek, Kurt. Hidden *Utah*. Berkeley, Calif.: Ulysses Press, 2000.

Sirvaitis, Karen. *Utah*. Minneapolis: Lerner Publications, 2002.

Steffof, Rebecca. *Utah*. Tarrytown, N.Y.: Marshall Cavendish Corporation, 2001.